Melodies of the Mind: Exploring Music Therapy

A. GITASHREE MAZUMDAR

notionpress
.com
INDIA · SINGAPORE · MALAYSIA

ISBN
Paperback 979-8-90007-835-9
Hardcase 979-8-90136-949-4

Acknowledgement

Writing *Melodies of the Mind: Exploring Music Therapy* has been a deeply fulfilling journey, and it would not have been possible without the unwavering support, encouragement, and inspiration from many individuals and institutions who have been part of my life.

First and foremost, I express my deepest gratitude to my beloved family. Your constant love, patience, and belief in me have been my greatest strength throughout this endeavour. To my daughters, **Gini, Mini & Mohor**—you are the light of my life and the inspiration behind every word of this book. I dedicate this work to you with all my heart. May you always find music in your lives and courage in your hearts.

I am profoundly grateful to my baba, **Pulak Majumdar**, and my ma, **Dipa Majumdar**, for guiding me onto the path of music and nurturing in me a deep love for this art. Along with their guidance, I cherish the artistic gene I inherited from my grandfather, **Amal Bhushan Majumdar**, a classical dancer whose legacy continues to inspire me.

To **Aniruddha Goswami**, my better half and dearest friend—thank you for being my unwavering pillar of support.

Your understanding and quiet strength have carried me through every challenge, and your belief in my dreams has meant more than words can express. This book is as much yours as it is mine.

Very special thanks to **Deboshree Bhattacharyya (didi)**, for being that light in the darkness. Your kindness, wisdom, and quiet encouragement came just when I needed it most. You reminded me to keep moving forward, and for that, I am deeply grateful. I am deeply thankful to **Soumyak Bhattacharyya (Dada)** for being a constant support.

I am sincerely thankful to my mentors who have guided me with their wisdom, insight and encouragement. Your teachings have shaped not only my professional journey but also my understanding of the transformative power of music therapy. Thank you for believing in my potential and nurturing my growth.

I extend my heartfelt appreciation to **Rabindra Bharati University (Kolkata)** for laying the academic foundation that shaped my understanding of music and its therapeutic dimensions. I am also grateful to the **Indian Music Therapy Association** for their pioneering efforts in promoting music therapy across the country and for fostering a supportive community of practitioners and scholars.

To all those who walk the path of healing—therapists, educators, caregivers, and seekers—I thank you for your tireless work and for reminding us every day that empathy and music can move mountains.

With profound gratitude,
– A. Gitashree Mazumdar

Preface

Music is often regarded as a universal language, transcending boundaries of language, culture, and time. It has the power to evoke emotions, trigger memories, and connect individuals across diverse backgrounds. But beyond its artistic and entertainment value, music has a deeper, therapeutic potential—one that can heal, transform, and support individuals in profound ways. This book, *Melodies of the Mind: Exploring Music Therapy*, is a journey into that potential, uncovering how sound, rhythm, and melody can become instruments of emotional, psychological, cognitive, and physical healing.

The idea of writing this book emerged from my years of exploration in the fields of psychology, music, and integrative therapies. As a music enthusiast and a student of human behaviour, I found myself constantly fascinated by how even a simple melody could evoke a wide spectrum of responses in people—from calmness and relaxation to deep emotional catharsis. Through academic study, clinical observation, and personal engagement with music, I witnessed how structured musical interventions could support individuals dealing with mental health issues, neurological conditions, developmental disorders, trauma, and much more. It became evident that music, when used therapeutically, has the power not just to entertain but to heal, regulate, and reconnect the fragmented parts of the self.

Melodies of the Mind is written for a wide audience – students of psychology and therapy, practising clinicians, educators, caregivers, and anyone curious about the therapeutic applications of music. This book aims to demystify the practice of music therapy, making it accessible and understandable even to those without a formal background in music. While rooted in theory and supported by research, the book maintains a practical tone throughout, offering tools, techniques, and real-world insights that can be applied in diverse settings.

The first chapter, *Introduction to Music Therapy*, provides a comprehensive overview of the origins, evolution, and foundational principles of the discipline. From its ancient roots to its emergence as a recognised clinical profession in the 20th century, music therapy has grown significantly in scope and methodology. This chapter also outlines the core definitions, roles of music therapists, and the ethical considerations involved in the practice.

In *Fundamentals of Music Therapy*, the second chapter, we delve into the theoretical underpinnings of how and why music works therapeutically. Drawing from neuroscience, psychology, and ethnomusicology, the chapter explains the physiological and psychological effects of music on the human brain and body. Concepts such as entrainment, auditory-motor coupling, emotional regulation, and neuroplasticity are discussed to provide readers with a scientific foundation.

Assessment is a crucial step in any therapeutic process, and *Chapter III: Assessment in Music Therapy* focuses on the tools and processes used to evaluate client needs, set goals, and track progress. This chapter includes standardised and non-standardised assessment strategies, and discusses how assessments are tailored for different age groups and clinical populations.

Chapters IV through VI explore the range of music therapy techniques used in practice. *Techniques for Different Populations* (Chapter IV) discusses how therapeutic interventions vary based on the needs of children, adolescents, adults, and the elderly, as well as populations with specific conditions like autism, dementia, or PTSD. This is followed by two chapters on core techniques: *Active Music Therapy Techniques* (Chapter V), which involve clients directly in music-making—through singing, playing instruments, songwriting, or improvisation—and *Receptive Music Therapy Techniques* (Chapter VI), which involve listening to music as a way to promote reflection, relaxation, or emotional release.

Chapter VII, *Integrative Techniques*, explores how music therapy can be combined with other therapeutic modalities such as cognitive-behavioural therapy (CBT), mindfulness-based practices, art therapy, and dance/movement therapy. Integration is a growing trend in modern psychotherapy, and music is particularly suited to blend with other modalities because of its flexibility and universal appeal.

In *Music Therapy in Different Settings* (Chapter VIII), we examine the application of music therapy in hospitals, schools, rehabilitation centres, hospices, mental health clinics, and community settings. Each environment poses unique challenges and opportunities, and this chapter offers insight into adapting the therapy to fit the context, resources, and client demographics.

Chapter IX: Practical Application and Case Study brings the theory to life. Through a detailed case study, readers can follow the process of assessment, intervention, and outcome in a real-world therapeutic scenario. This chapter provides a model for understanding the nuanced decision-making, creativity, and adaptability required in music therapy practice.

Finally, *Chapter X: Music Therapy for Specific Populations* offers focused insights into working with individuals dealing with trauma, neurodivergence, terminal illness, substance use disorders, and more. These sections emphasise cultural sensitivity, trauma-informed care, and individualised approaches.

As with any therapeutic discipline, music therapy is a dynamic and evolving field. While this book offers a solid foundation, it also encourages ongoing learning, collaboration, and exploration. The field continues to grow as research unveils more about the brain's response to music and as therapists innovate to meet the changing needs of society. My hope is that this book inspires its readers to not only understand music therapy but to engage with it—whether as practitioners, advocates, or beneficiaries.

To those already working in healing professions, I invite you to consider music not just as an adjunct but as a potent, standalone modality capable of unlocking emotional and cognitive doors that words alone often cannot. To music lovers, this book might offer a new lens through which to appreciate the depth of what music can offer. And to those who may be struggling with emotional or psychological challenges, I hope this book brings the reassuring message that healing can come from even the softest hum, the simplest rhythm, the quietest melody.

In closing, *Melodies of the Mind* is both an academic and heartfelt endeavour. It is grounded in evidence but born from the belief that healing is not always linear, not always verbal, and not always visible—but it is always possible. Through music, we reconnect with our emotions, our memories, and most importantly, with each other.

– A. Gitashree Mazumdar

Contents

I

Introduction to Music Therapy

Definition of Indian Music Therapy

Indian music therapy is a form of therapeutic intervention that uses the principles, techniques, and specific elements of Indian classical music to promote physical, mental, emotional, and spiritual well-being. It involves the use of ragas (melodic frameworks), talas (rhythmic patterns), and other elements of Indian music to achieve therapeutic goals, such as reducing stress, improving mood, enhancing cognitive function, and promoting overall health.

In Indian music, we have different types of music which can be used. They are.

- **Ragas**: Melodic frameworks that are believed to have specific emotional and physiological effects on the listener. Each raga is associated with certain times of the day and specific moods.

- **Talas**: Rhythmic cycles that structure the musical composition and can influence the body's natural rhythms.
- **Nada Yoga**: The ancient practice of sound meditation and the use of sound vibrations for healing and spiritual growth.
- **Chanting and Mantras**: The use of repetitive sounds or phrases to create therapeutic effects and alter states of consciousness.

History of Indian Music Therapy

- **Vedic Period**: The origins of Indian music therapy can be traced back to the Vedic period, where the chanting of hymns and mantras was an integral part of rituals and healing practices. The Vedas, ancient sacred texts, emphasise the importance of sound and its therapeutic potential.
- **Sama Veda**: One of the four Vedas, the Sama Veda, is particularly focused on musical chanting. It is believed that the hymns of the Sama Veda have healing properties and can create a sense of harmony and balance.
- **Natya Shastra**: Written by Bharata Muni, this ancient treatise on performing arts includes detailed descriptions of music, dance, and drama. It explores the emotional and psychological effects of different musical modes and rhythms.
- **Bhakti and Sufi Movements**: During the medieval period, devotional music in the form of bhajans (Hindu devotional songs) and qawwalis (Sufi devotional songs) played a significant role in healing and spiritual practices.

- **Rabindranath Tagore**: The Nobel laureate poet and musician emphasised the therapeutic potential of music in education and healing. Rabindra Sangeet is very famous among a sect of Indian people. The Bengalis usually use this genre of music in every aspect of life.
- **Pandit Vishnu Narayan Bhatkhande and Pandit Vishnu Digambar Paluskar**: These early 20th-century musicologists helped to systematise and revitalise Indian classical music, indirectly contributing to its therapeutic applications.
- **Bollywood Songs & Other Regional Language Songs:** The Bollywood genre of songs, along with regional language songs, also have a huge variation to be used in music therapy purposes, as they provide songs of all emotions and can be used effectively in passive music therapy sessions.

Benefits of Music Therapy

1. Music therapy can help reduce the perception of pain, alleviate discomfort, and improve pain management.
2. Music therapy can enhance fine and gross motor skills, especially in individuals with physical disabilities or after a stroke.
3. Listening to soothing music can help lower heart rate and blood pressure, contributing to overall cardiovascular health.
4. It can motivate patients during physical therapy exercises, making the process more enjoyable and effective.
5. Music therapy can significantly reduce stress and anxiety levels, promoting relaxation and emotional well-being.

6. Engaging with music can elevate mood, reduce symptoms of depression, and provide a sense of joy and fulfilment.
7. It provides a safe outlet for expressing complex emotions and can help individuals process and understand their feelings.
8. Music therapy can enhance memory recall, particularly beneficial for individuals with Alzheimer's disease or other forms of dementia.
9. It can stimulate cognitive functions, aiding in attention, executive function, and problem-solving skills.
10. Music can facilitate learning by improving focus and retention of information.
11. Music therapy can enhance verbal and non-verbal communication, especially in individuals with speech or language impairments.
12. Participating in music therapy sessions can foster social interaction, cooperation, and relationship-building.
13. Group music therapy sessions can create a sense of community and belonging, reducing feelings of isolation and loneliness.
14. Music therapy can aid in the development of social skills, motor skills, and cognitive functions in children, including those with developmental disorders such as autism.
15. For older adults, it can improve cognitive function, provide social engagement, and enhance quality of life.
16. It is effective in treating various mental health conditions, including depression, anxiety, PTSD, and substance abuse disorders.

17. In medical settings, music therapy can support patients undergoing surgery, those in palliative care, and individuals coping with chronic illnesses.

Science Behind Music Therapy

Music has been used as a healing tool since ancient times across cultures. In Indian traditions, references to the therapeutic role of music are found in the Vedas and Nātyaśāstra. Modern music therapy, though, is increasingly supported by a growing body of scientific research from disciplines such as neuroscience, psychology, physiology, and cognitive science. This chapter explores the scientific foundations behind music therapy and aligns them with the ancient Indian understanding of sound and healing.

Neuroscience of Music Therapy

a. Brain Regions Activated by Music

- Music activates multiple brain areas simultaneously, including the auditory cortex, prefrontal cortex (emotional regulation), amygdala (emotions), hippocampus (memory), and motor cortex (rhythm and movement).
- Imaging techniques like fMRI and PET scans reveal how music can modulate brain circuits involved in reward, stress, and social bonding.

b. Neurochemical Effects

- Music increases levels of dopamine (pleasure), oxytocin (bonding), and endorphins (pain relief).

- It reduces cortisol, a hormone linked with stress, thereby supporting mental health.

c. Neuroplasticity

- Regular exposure to music can promote neural plasticity—strengthening connections and rewiring pathways. This is significant in rehabilitation, stroke recovery, and neurodevelopmental disorders like autism.

Physiological Effects of Music

a. Cardiovascular and Respiratory Systems

- Music can entrain the heartbeat and breathing, a principle mirrored in Indian practices using *nada yoga* and *pranayama* with musical intonation.
- Slow-tempo music tends to lower heart rate and blood pressure, while faster rhythms can energise and stimulate.

b. Pain Modulation

- Music activates descending pain modulatory pathways, thereby reducing perceived pain without pharmaceuticals.
- Studies show patients undergoing surgery or chemotherapy report lower pain and anxiety levels when exposed to specific musical interventions.

Psychological and Cognitive Effects

a. Mood and Emotion Regulation

- Music influences affective states and is used to treat conditions like depression, anxiety, PTSD, and insomnia.

- Emotional expression and processing through music help in trauma resolution, grief, and personal insight.

b. Cognitive Enhancement

- Music improves attention, memory recall, and executive functioning. In Alzheimer's patients, familiar music often rekindles memories.
- Rhythmic auditory stimulation (RAS) aids in improving gait and coordination in Parkinson's disease patients.

Scientific Understanding of Indian Music Therapy

Indian music therapy often relies on *rāga chikitsā*—the therapeutic application of specific rāgas. While rooted in tradition, these approaches align with modern scientific principles:

a. Rāga and Emotion

- Rāgas are structured in specific *thāts* (modes) and *rasas* (emotions). EEG and ECG studies show different rāgas induce distinct emotional and physiological responses.
- E.g., Rāga Darbari Kanada evokes calm and lowers stress, while Rāga Bhairavi may uplift mood.

b. Tonal and Temporal Elements

- Time theory of rāga (singing rāgas at specific times of the day) may correlate with circadian rhythms, a concept also studied in chronotherapy (timing treatment).

c. Mantras and Nāda Yoga

- Chanting and drone-based practices (a long continuous note, which you can use as a backing track for music practice) - particularly those involving the tanpura—have been shown to influence brainwave entrainment by promoting alpha (8–12 Hz) and theta (4–8 Hz) frequency states. These frequencies are neurologically linked to states of deep relaxation, focused meditation, and therapeutic healing. The sustained harmonic resonance of the tanpura creates a stable auditory environment, allowing the brain to synchronise with slower rhythms, facilitating mental stillness and emotional regulation. Mantra chanting, when combined with the tonal backdrop of a drone, further enhances this effect by introducing rhythmic vocalisation and breath control, both of which are known to reduce sympathetic nervous system activity and promote parasympathetic dominance—key for stress reduction and healing responses (Kumar, Telles, & Nagendra, 1999).

Evidence-Based Applications

Condition	Music Therapy Effect	Supporting Study
Depression	Mood improvement, emotional processing	Harvard Health, 2020
Dementia	Memory recall via familiar melodies	Särkämö et al., 2014

Condition	Music Therapy Effect	Supporting Study
Autism	Social interaction, speech improvement	Geretsegger et al., 2014
Hypertension	Blood pressure regulation via classical rāgas	Indian Journal of Physiology and Pharmacology, 2012

Integration of Tradition and Science

While Indian music therapy has a deeply spiritual and holistic foundation, its efficacy is increasingly validated through modern scientific methods. By aligning the *nāda* (sound) and *bhava* (emotion) of Indian rāgas with neurophysiological outcomes, practitioners can offer a blended approach of tradition and evidence-based healing.

Music therapy rests on a solid scientific foundation, with measurable effects on the brain, body, and mind. Indian music therapy, with its rich cultural, emotional, and spiritual dimensions, provides an even deeper canvas for healing. Understanding the science behind music enables therapists to bridge the gap between ancient wisdom and contemporary clinical practice.

II

Fundamentals of Music Therapy

Music therapists play a crucial role in healthcare and therapeutic settings by using music as a tool to address the physical, emotional, cognitive, and social needs of individuals.

1. **Assessment**: Music therapists assess the needs and abilities of their clients. This includes understanding their physical health, emotional well-being, cognitive functioning, communication abilities, and social skills.
2. **Therapeutic Planning**: Based on the assessment, music therapists develop individualised treatment plans. These plans outline specific goals and objectives tailored to the client's needs.
3. **Implementation of Therapy**: Music therapists use various music-based interventions to work towards the goals set in the treatment plan. These interventions can include playing instruments, singing, and songwriting, listening to music, and engaging in music-based activities.

4. **Emotional Expression and Processing**: Music therapy can help clients express and process their emotions in a non-verbal way. This is particularly useful for individuals who have difficulty expressing themselves through words.
5. **Cognitive Rehabilitation**: For individuals with cognitive impairments, music therapy can enhance memory, attention, and executive functioning. Activities such as learning new songs, playing instruments, and participating in rhythm-based exercises can stimulate cognitive processes.
6. **Physical Rehabilitation**: Music therapy can support physical rehabilitation by improving motor skills, coordination, and movement. Rhythm and music can be used to enhance physical activities and exercises.
7. **Social Interaction**: Music therapy provides opportunities for social interaction, helping clients develop and improve their social skills. Group music therapy sessions can foster a sense of community and belonging.
8. **Stress Reduction and Relaxation**: Music therapy can promote relaxation and reduce stress. Techniques such as guided imagery with music, music-assisted relaxation, and listening to calming music can help lower anxiety levels.
9. **Pain Management**: Music therapy can be an effective tool for managing pain. Listening to music, especially preferred or soothing music, can distract from pain and promote a sense of comfort.
10. **Support in Mental Health Treatment**: Music therapists work with individuals experiencing mental health issues such as depression, anxiety, PTSD, and schizophrenia.

Music therapy can provide a safe space for self-expression, emotional release, and coping.

11. **Collaboration with Other Professionals**: Music therapists often work as part of a multidisciplinary team, collaborating with doctors, nurses, psychologists, physical therapists, occupational therapists, and other healthcare professionals to provide comprehensive care.
12. **Research and Advocacy**: Music therapists engage in research to explore the benefits of music therapy and contribute to the evidence base of the field. They also advocate for the inclusion of music therapy in various healthcare settings and promote its benefits to the broader community.

III

Assessment in Music Therapy

Initial Assessment Techniques in Music Therapy

Initial Assessment in Music Therapy is a crucial step in understanding a client's needs, preferences, and baseline functioning. The process often involves several techniques to gather information that will guide the therapy process. Common initial assessment techniques are –

a. **Interview and Background Information**

   Interviews are conducted to gather relevant personal, medical and social history of the client. Usually, interviews are conducted by conversing with the client or the caregivers to understand their history, cultural background, interests in music, etc.

b. **Observation**

   Observation is the method in which we need to observe the client's behaviour, mood and responses in a natural setting.

This can be done by observing the client during a session, or by playing two genres of music to see how they react.

c. **Musical Interaction**

This helps to understand the client's musical abilities, preferences and how they engage in music. This can be assessed by engaging the client in a series of activities such as singing, playing instruments, improvisation or listening to music. This helps the therapist to assess rhythm, pitch, tempo and emotional responses to music.

d. **Clinical Music Improvisation**

The purpose of this assessment is to evaluate spontaneous musical creativity and emotional expression. The therapist and client engage in improvised music-making. The therapist observes how the client improvises, their level of creativity, and their emotional and cognitive responses during the improvisation.

Ongoing Therapy Assessment Methods

a. **Observational assessment**

The therapist observes the client's behaviours, responses, and interactions during music therapy sessions. This includes noting changes in mood, blood pressure, and pulse rate, physical movement, social engagement, and emotional expressions. The client's engagement with music, such as rhythm, melody, and tempo, is closely monitored. How a client is interacting with music can provide insights into their emotional and psychological state.

b. Client feedback

Client feedback can be in two ways: verbal and non-verbal feedback. In verbal feedback, the therapist encourages clients to share their thoughts and feelings about the sessions. This direct feedback can guide the direction of future sessions. For clients who may not express verbally, therapists can pay attention to non-verbal cues like facial expressions, body language, and eye contact.

c. Pre-, post- and during-session assessments

Pre-Session: Pre-session helps to establish baseline information about the client's emotional, cognitive, physical, and social state. It also determines therapeutic goals based on the client's needs. It may involve observation, interviews, or standardised tools.

During Session: There is a continuous evaluation of the client's responses and engagement during music therapy. Adjustments are made to the intervention based on real-time feedback. Focus on emotional expression, physical movement, verbal interaction, etc.

Post-Session Assessment: Reviews and reflects on the session's outcomes. It also helps to compare pre-session goals with actual progress and guides future sessions by refining goals and strategies based on observed changes.

d. Goal-oriented evaluation

Therapists often set specific, measurable, achievable, relevant and time-bound (SMART) goals with clients at the beginning of therapy. Progress towards these goals is regularly reviewed to determine the effectiveness of the interventions.

These are specific indicators such as improved communication skills, reduced anxiety, or enhanced social interaction, which are tracked over time.

e. **Tools and instruments of assessment in Music Therapy**

In music therapy, various tools and instruments are used to assess clients' needs, preferences, and progress. These tools help music therapists understand the client's emotional, cognitive, social, and physical status, allowing them to tailor their interventions effectively.

Observation Tools

a. **Behaviour Observation Forms**: These forms are used to record specific behaviours during music therapy sessions, such as engagement, eye contact, and social interaction.

b. **Therapist's Notes**: Detailed notes taken by the therapist during and after sessions to track the client's progress, reactions, and any significant changes in behaviour.

Musical Tools and Instruments

a. **Improvisational Assessment:** The therapist uses instruments or the client's voice to improvise music, assessing the client's ability to express emotions, interact, and respond to musical cues.

b. **Songwriting/Composition:** Clients may be asked to write or compose music, which is then analysed to understand their cognitive and emotional state.

c. **Instrumental Play:** The choice and manner in which clients play instruments can reveal much about their emotional well-being, motor skills, and cognitive functions.

d. **Voice and Singing Assessments:** Assessing a client's use of voice, including pitch, tone, and rhythm, can provide insights into their emotional state and neurological functioning.

Collaborative Assessments

a. **Family and Caregiver Interviews**: Gathering information from family members or caregivers to get a broader understanding of the client's behaviour and needs outside therapy sessions.

b. **Multidisciplinary Team Assessments**: Collaboration with other healthcare professionals to create a comprehensive assessment plan that considers all aspects of the client's health.

Case Study: Music Therapy for a Child Facing Gaming Addiction

Background: Rohan (Name changed), a 12-year-old boy, has been struggling with excessive gaming addiction for the past two years. His parents became concerned when his daily gaming hours exceeded 6-8 hours, significantly impacting his school performance, social interactions, and overall well-being. Rohan often displayed irritability, restlessness, and anxiety when not gaming, and his sleep schedule was highly disrupted.

After multiple attempts to reduce screen time and introduce alternative activities, his parents sought professional help. A therapist suggested incorporating music therapy as part of a comprehensive treatment plan, aiming to help Rohan develop healthier coping mechanisms and reduce his dependence on gaming.

Therapeutic Goals:

Reduce gaming time and increase engagement in alternative activities.

Improve emotional regulation and reduce anxiety associated with not gaming.

Enhance social skills through collaborative music-making activities.

Promote self-expression and self-awareness, helping Rohan identify emotions and triggers related to his gaming addiction.

Music Therapy Intervention:

Initial Assessment: The music therapist conducted an initial assessment to understand Rohan's musical preferences, interests, and emotional responses to different types of music. It was noted that Rohan enjoyed fast-paced, energetic music similar to the background music found in many of his favourite video games. This insight was used to design interventions that would gradually introduce him to a broader range of musical experiences.

Creating a Safe Space: In the early sessions, the therapist focused on building a rapport with Rohan and creating a safe and comfortable environment. Simple rhythmic exercises using drums, a clap box, and percussion instruments were introduced to engage him physically and emotionally. Rohan responded well to these exercises, finding them fun and engaging.

Musical Storytelling: To encourage self-expression, the therapist used a technique called musical storytelling. Rohan was asked to create a story based on his experiences, feelings, or interests, and then express that story through sound using various instruments. This activity helped him externalise his emotions and gain insight into his thoughts about gaming and its impact on his life.

Songwriting and Lyric Analysis: The therapist introduced songwriting sessions where Rohan was guided to write lyrics about his feelings, experiences, and challenges related to gaming. He explored themes of frustration, excitement, and anxiety. Together with the therapist, Rohan analysed the lyrics of songs that resonated with him, identifying how certain music styles and lyrics influenced his mood and behaviour.

Mindfulness Through Music: Sessions included mindfulness exercises paired with calming, slow-tempo music. This was aimed at helping Rohan develop relaxation techniques and cope with feelings of anxiety or withdrawal when not gaming. Gradually, Rohan learned to use music as a tool for emotional regulation, particularly during moments of craving or frustration.

Group Music-Making: To improve social skills and reduce isolation, the therapist invited Rohan to participate in group music-making sessions with other children. These sessions involved collaborative activities like drum circles, group improvisation, and simple ensemble playing. Rohan found enjoyment and satisfaction in these interactions, discovering a new sense of connection and fulfilment.

Gradual Exposure and Substitution: The therapist used Rohan's interest in energetic music and gaming soundtracks as a starting point to introduce other musical genres. For example, instead of the fast-paced tracks he was used to, they experimented with rhythmic complexity or instrumental diversity. This broadened Rohan's musical palette and offered new ways to engage with music that did not involve screens.

Outcomes:

Reduction in Gaming Hours: Over a 3-month period, Rohan's gaming hours reduced from 8 hours per day to approximately 2-3 hours per day. He began to engage more in music-related activities and showed interest in learning the guitar.

Improved Emotional Regulation: Rohan learned to recognise his feelings of anxiety and craving. He started using music and rhythmic exercises to manage these emotions, which led to decreased irritability and mood swings.

Enhanced Social Interactions: Rohan showed increased confidence in group settings and was more willing to interact with peers outside of gaming environments. His participation in group music sessions fostered teamwork, listening skills, and empathy.

Development of New Interests: Rohan's interest in music expanded beyond therapy sessions. He expressed a desire to join a local music club, demonstrating a new area of interest that replaced some of his gaming time.

Family Involvement and Support: The therapist included Rohan's family in the sessions by encouraging them to participate in musical activities at home, fostering a supportive environment for change.

Conclusion: Music therapy proved to be an effective intervention for Rohan's gaming addiction. It provided him with a creative outlet for self-expression, a means to manage emotions, and an alternative source of enjoyment and connection. The holistic approach helped him reduce his dependence on gaming and build new, healthier habits.

This case illustrates how music therapy can be tailored to meet the specific needs of children facing behavioural challenges, such as gaming addiction, by leveraging their existing interests while gradually introducing healthier alternatives.

IV

Techniques for Different Age Groups

Music therapy is a powerful tool that can be tailored to suit people of all ages. The techniques used in music therapy vary depending on the age group, developmental stage, and the specific needs of the individuals.

1. Infants and Toddlers (0-3 years)

Lullabies and Soothing Music: Soft, gentle lullabies are used to help with relaxation, sleep, and emotional bonding between the caregiver and the child.

Rhythmic Movement and Singing: Singing and simple rhythmic movements (like clapping or tapping) are used to promote sensory integration, motor development, and emotional expression.

Instrument Play: Simple instruments like drums, shakers, and bells encourage sensory exploration and motor skills while enhancing auditory discrimination.

Vocal Play and Mimicking Sounds: Encourages language development and social interaction by mimicking sounds, babbling, or singing simple songs.

2. Preschool Children (3-6 years)

Action Songs and Rhythmic Games: These encourage motor coordination, listening skills, and memory. Songs with actions like "The Wheels on the Bus" or "Chanda mama dur ke" help with language and cognitive development.

Improvisation and Musical Storytelling: Using music to tell stories or express emotions helps children develop creativity, language, and social-emotional skills.

Instrumental Exploration: Playing different instruments helps with motor development, hand-eye coordination, and sensory processing.

Music and Movement Activities: Combining music with dance or movement helps children develop body awareness, spatial orientation, and social skills.

3. Children (7-12 years)

Lyric Analysis and Songwriting: Encourages children to express their feelings, thoughts, and experiences, which can be especially useful for children dealing with emotional or behavioural challenges.

Musical Games and Group Music-Making: Promote social skills, teamwork, and cooperation. Activities like group drumming or choral singing encourage peer interaction.

Improvisation and Composition: Allows children to create their own music, fostering creativity, self-expression, and confidence.

4. Adolescents (13-18 years)

Songwriting and Lyric Discussion: Writing and analysing song lyrics provide an outlet for self-expression, identity exploration, and emotional processing.

Rap Therapy: Engages adolescents by using music genres they relate to, allowing them to express emotions, thoughts, and experiences creatively.

Improvisational Music-Making: Encourages spontaneity, decision-making, and emotional expression. Group improvisation can also enhance social skills.

Music for Relaxation and Stress Reduction: Techniques like guided imagery with music, deep listening, or playing instruments help reduce anxiety and improve mood.

5. Adults (18-65 years)

Guided Imagery and Music (GIM): Involves listening to music in a relaxed state to evoke images, feelings, and memories, helping adults explore emotions and improve mental health.

Lyric Analysis and Song Discussion: Encourages discussion of personal experiences, emotional processing, and building coping skills.

Instrumental and Vocal Improvisation: Provides an outlet for emotional release and self-expression, promoting self-awareness and emotional regulation.

Community Music Therapy: Engages adults in group music-making activities to foster social connections, reduce isolation, and promote a sense of belonging.

6. Older Adults (65+ years)

Reminiscence and Life Review through Music: Involves listening to or singing songs from the individual's past to stimulate memories, promote social interaction, and enhance self-esteem.

Music and Movement for Physical Rehabilitation: Combines music with movement to improve physical coordination, balance, and motor skills. This is particularly useful in dementia and Parkinson's disease.

Singing for Cognitive and Emotional Support: Singing familiar songs can help maintain cognitive function, improve mood, and provide comfort for those with Alzheimer's or other forms of dementia.

Relaxation Techniques: Use of calming music to reduce anxiety, agitation, and pain, and to promote relaxation and improve sleep.

7. Individuals with Special Needs (All Ages)

Adaptive Music Lessons: Tailored music lessons that accommodate the individual's abilities, enhancing their self-esteem, social skills, and cognitive functioning.

Music for Sensory Integration: Using various sounds, rhythms, and instruments to help individuals with sensory processing disorders improve sensory modulation.

Music-Assisted Communication: Utilises music to enhance communication skills in individuals with non-verbal autism, speech impairments, or other communication disorders.

Rhythmic Auditory Stimulation: A technique used to improve motor function, particularly in those with neurological conditions like stroke or cerebral palsy.

V

Active Music Therapy Techniques

Active music therapy involves the client actively engaging in the creation or performance of music as a means of therapeutic expression and healing. Below is an elaboration on key active music therapy techniques:

Improvisation

Improvisation in music therapy involves the spontaneous creation of music without pre-composed material, offering a way to express thoughts, feelings, or emotions in a non-verbal form. This technique is often used to facilitate emotional release, self-expression, or communication, especially for those who may struggle with verbal expression.

Techniques & Methods

Free Improvisation: The client is encouraged to play or sing freely without structure or guidance. This open-ended method promotes self-discovery and emotional exploration.

Structured Improvisation: The therapist might give a basic framework, such as a specific rhythm, melody, or theme, within which the client can improvise. This can help build confidence and focus the session.

Call-and-Response: The therapist plays a musical phrase, and the client responds with their own improvisation, fostering communication and interaction.

Dialogic Improvisation: A musical "conversation" takes place between therapist and client, allowing them to express emotions or ideas through music.

Instruments & Equipment

Percussion Instruments: Drums, tambourines and maracas are commonly used, allowing for non-melodic and rhythmic exploration.

Piano or Keyboard: Provides harmonic and melodic opportunities for improvisation.

Guitar: Used for both rhythm and melody, and it is portable, making it versatile for different settings.

Voice: Singing or vocalising sounds can be a powerful way to express emotions.

Composition

Composition in music therapy allows clients to express themselves by creating original songs or musical pieces. It can be particularly effective in processing emotions, telling stories, or improving cognitive and creative skills.

Songwriting

Lyric Writing: Clients create their own lyrics, which can reflect their personal experiences, emotions, or therapeutic goals. The therapist guides them in shaping these into a coherent song.

Melody Creation: Clients might compose their own melodies, which can be as simple or complex as their skills allow. This process helps to channel emotional expression into structured musical forms.

Collaborative Composition: In a group setting, clients may work together to create a song or musical piece. This fosters teamwork, communication, and a sense of community.

Collaborative Composition

Therapist-Client Collaboration: The therapist may collaborate with the client, offering suggestions and support during the songwriting process. This dynamic can build trust and help the client feel supported.

Group Composition: In a therapeutic group setting, participants may work together to write lyrics, create a melody, and compose a full song. This promotes social interaction, creativity, and a shared sense of accomplishment.

Re-creation

Re-creation involves covering or performing existing music, often songs that are meaningful or familiar to the client. This technique helps develop musical skills, boost confidence, and offer an emotional connection to familiar songs.

Covering & Performing Existing Music

Singing Familiar Songs: Clients sing along to songs they already know, helping them tap into memories, emotions, and self-expression. This is particularly useful for clients with memory or cognitive challenges, such as those with Alzheimer's or dementia.

Instrumental Re-Creation: Clients play existing music on an instrument, which can enhance motor skills, focus and concentration.

Karaoke Therapy: Some therapists use karaoke as a way for clients to engage with music, express emotions, and boost self-esteem.

Adaptation for Therapeutic Purposes

Adaptation is the process of modifying musical activities or instruments to suit the therapeutic needs of clients. This might involve adjusting the key of a song, simplifying rhythms, or using specially designed instruments that are easier to play for those with physical or cognitive limitations.

Therapeutic Adaptation Techniques

Simplifying Music: Songs or melodies may be simplified to make them accessible for clients with limited musical experience or cognitive abilities. For example, slowing down the tempo or changing the key to accommodate a client's vocal range.

Custom Instruments: Instruments can be adapted for individuals with physical disabilities. For example, large drum mallets might be used for clients with limited motor skills, or electronic instruments that can be played with minimal movement.

Adjusting Themes: The content of songs or music might be adjusted to reflect therapeutic goals, such as selecting songs that focus on resilience, hope, or other relevant themes.

In all cases, the music therapist innovates techniques to the unique needs and goals of the client, whether it's emotional healing, cognitive rehabilitation, or social development.

VI

Receptive Techniques of Music Therapy

Receptive Music Therapy Techniques

Receptive music therapy refers to interventions where clients listen to music as a therapeutic process, rather than actively creating it themselves. These techniques are commonly used to promote emotional expression, relaxation, self-awareness, and psychological healing. Below are two key receptive techniques: Music Listening (Guided Imagery in Music) and Lyrics Analysis.

Music Listening (Guided Imagery in Music)

This technique involves the therapeutic use of pre-recorded or live music to evoke images, emotions, and memories, often facilitated by a therapist. Guided imagery is a specific form of music listening used for relaxation, stress reduction, emotional exploration, and insight into personal experiences.

Guided Imagery and Music (GIM):

Definition: GIM is a method in which clients listen to music while guided by a therapist to explore their subconscious thoughts and emotions. Developed by Helen Bonny, it often uses classical or instrumental music.

Process: The client relaxes and listens to a carefully selected piece of music. The therapist encourages the client to share the images, emotions, or thoughts that arise during the session. The therapist helps the client interpret and explore these images, which may represent subconscious emotions, memories, or unresolved conflicts. This exploration can lead to insights about emotional challenges, psychological blocks, or life patterns.

Relaxation and Stress Reduction:

How it Works: The therapist may choose specific music that is slow-tempo, soft, and gentle to induce relaxation and a meditative state. The music acts as a tool to regulate breathing, lower heart rate, and reduce muscle tension.

Outcome: As the music plays, clients often experience deep relaxation, reduced stress, and mental clarity, which can help them better cope with anxiety, chronic stress, or emotional distress.

Common Uses: Music listening for relaxation is frequently used with individuals suffering from anxiety, PTSD, chronic pain, or high stress levels.

Psychological Insight: Through GIM, clients might gain insight into repressed emotions or unresolved conflicts. The music acts as a bridge to deep emotional material, providing a safe space for exploration.

Example: A person with chronic anxiety might listen to calming instrumental music while their therapist guides them to imagine a peaceful place. The imagery that arises could reveal deeper emotional needs, like a desire for security or control, leading to a broader therapeutic discussion.

Lyrics Analysis (Exploring and Discussing Lyrics)

Lyrics analysis is another receptive music therapy technique where clients and therapists explore the meaning behind the lyrics of a song and relate them to the client's personal life experiences. This can help the client gain insight into their emotions, identify coping strategies, and facilitate personal growth.

Exploring and Discussing Lyrics:

In lyrics analysis, the therapist selects songs with lyrics that might resonate with the client's situation, emotions, or experiences. Together, they explore and discuss the meaning of the lyrics.

Therapeutic Goals: Facilitating emotional expression. Providing insight into personal thoughts and behaviours. Building empathy and self-awareness. Encouraging cognitive reframing, where clients can reinterpret negative experiences in a more positive or productive way.

How it Works: The client listens to a song. The therapist asks open-ended questions like, "What part of the song stood out to you?" or "How do you connect to these lyrics?" The client shares their interpretation and personal connections, which can reveal underlying emotions or thoughts.

Connecting Lyrics to Personal Experiences:

***Emotional Expression*:** Lyrics often contain themes of love, loss, joy or pain, making them relatable. By discussing the emotions that resonate with the client, they may find it easier to express feelings they otherwise struggle to express.

Exploring Life Events: The lyrics may act as a metaphor or mirror for the client's own life events, such as breakups, grief, or personal achievements. Through this lens, clients can explore the emotions associated with these events in a non-threatening way.

Identifying Coping Strategies: Lyrics can provide validation of the client's feelings and struggles, showing them they are not alone. They may also identify coping strategies or new ways of thinking based on the lyrics, which can help with their personal healing journey.

Strengthening Self-Identity: The process of reflecting on lyrics often strengthens clients' self-awareness and self-identity as they relate the song's themes to their own personality, values, and life circumstances.

Example: A client going through a tough breakup might analyse a song with lyrics about heartbreak and resilience. In discussing the song's message, they might express their own feelings of sadness, frustration, or hope, and even gain clarity about how to move forward or redefine their identity post-breakup.

VII

Integrative Techniques (Combining With Music Therapy)

Integrative techniques that combine music with other therapeutic modalities like art therapy, dance and movement therapy, and drama therapy offer a holistic approach to healing. These approaches allow individuals to express themselves in creative ways that can complement traditional verbal therapies. Below is an overview of how music integrates with each of these therapies:

Music and Art Therapy: Art Therapy uses the creative process of making art to improve a person's mental, emotional, and physical well-being. When integrated with Music Therapy, the combination can deepen the therapeutic experience, engage multiple senses and encourage emotional expression through both sound and visuals.

How It Works:

Simultaneous Expression: Clients create visual artwork while listening to music, which may evoke specific emotions or memories. Music can help stimulate creativity and inspire the art-making process.

Symbolic Connection: After creating art while listening to music, individuals can discuss the emotions or thoughts both mediums helped evoke, deepening self-awareness.

Therapeutic Goals: The combination helps people process difficult emotions like trauma, grief, or anxiety, as both music and visual art bypass verbal expression, allowing for a non-verbal release of emotions.

Music and Dance/Movement Therapy (DMT):

Dance/Movement Therapy is based on the idea that movement and emotion are interconnected, using body movements to enhance emotional, cognitive, and physical health. When paired with Music Therapy, movement becomes a more powerful tool for healing.

How It Works:

Rhythmic Synchronisation: Music naturally encourages movement, and when used in dance therapy, it can facilitate freer expression. The body responds to the rhythm, tone, and tempo of music, aiding in the release of emotional blockages.

Emotional Expression: Some emotions are difficult to express verbally, but music paired with movement allows for non-verbal emotional expression. This can be helpful in dealing with anxiety, depression, or trauma, where words may fail.

Mind-Body Connection: The combination of music and movement encourages mindfulness, grounding individuals in the present moment, which can promote relaxation, stress reduction, and emotional regulation.

Music and Drama Therapy:

Drama Therapy uses role-playing, storytelling, and improvisation to explore personal experiences, challenges, and emotions. Music enhances the dramatic elements by adding songs or rhythm, supporting emotional exploration and expression.

How It Works:

Musical Improvisation: In drama therapy, musical improvisation can be used to enhance storytelling or role-playing. For instance, a therapist may play a particular melody or rhythm that resonates with the emotions the client is portraying in a role.

Songwriting and Role Play: Clients might write songs or engage in role-play exercises that incorporate music, allowing them to express complex emotional experiences in a safe and creative way.

Emotional Resonance: Music can help set the emotional tone for the dramatic exercise, guiding participants into deeper emotional states or helping them feel more connected to the characters or scenarios they are exploring.

Benefits of Integrating Music with Other Therapies:

Multisensory Engagement: Engaging multiple senses (sound, movement, sight) can create a more profound therapeutic experience, particularly for those who struggle with traditional talk therapies.

Enhanced Emotional Release: Music facilitates emotional expression and can evoke feelings that may be buried, which other creative therapies like dance or art can further explore.

Greater Flexibility: These integrative approaches are adaptable for different populations (children, adults, trauma survivors, individuals with disabilities, etc.).

Strengthened Therapeutic Alliance: The creative process in these therapies often fosters trust and connection between client and therapist, as it is collaborative and non-judgemental.

VIII

Music Therapy in Different Settings

Music therapy is a versatile therapeutic approach used in a variety of settings to promote physical, emotional, cognitive and social well-being. Its adaptability makes it valuable across several domains, including medical, educational and private practice environments.

Hospital & Medical Settings

In hospitals and medical settings, music therapy is often integrated into treatment plans to aid patients in coping with physical and emotional challenges. Music therapy in these settings may include the following:

- **Pain Management**: Music therapy can reduce the perception of pain in patients, helping them manage discomfort without relying solely on medication. It is used in areas such as post-operative recovery, cancer care, and chronic pain treatment.

- **Stress and Anxiety Reduction**: Music therapy helps alleviate stress and anxiety, especially in pre- and post-surgical procedures, intensive care units (ICUs), and during treatments such as chemotherapy. For example, calming music has been shown to lower blood pressure, slow heart rates, and reduce the need for sedatives.
- **Neonatal Intensive Care Units (NICUs)**: In NICUs, music therapy has been used to improve preterm infants' vital signs, promote feeding, and enhance bonding with parents through the use of lullabies and gentle rhythms.
- **Rehabilitation and Physical Recovery**: In rehabilitation, music is used to enhance motor skills and coordination, particularly for stroke survivors, traumatic brain injury (TBI) patients, and those recovering from surgery. Rhythm-based exercises can improve movement and coordination.
- **Emotional and Psychological Support**: For patients dealing with serious illness or end-of-life care (palliative care or hospice), music therapy offers emotional support, helping them process their feelings, reduce isolation, and improve overall mood.

Educational Settings

Music therapy in schools and other educational settings is an effective way to support children's academic, emotional, and social development. In these settings, music therapy programmes often focus on:

- **Special Education**: Music therapy is commonly used with students who have developmental, intellectual, or learning disabilities, such as autism spectrum disorder (ASD),

Down syndrome, or ADHD. The structured use of music can help improve attention, communication skills, social interaction, and cognitive functioning.

- **Emotional and Behavioural Regulation**: Music therapy is used to support students who struggle with emotional regulation, anxiety, depression, or behavioural disorders. Therapeutic music activities provide a healthy outlet for expressing feelings and managing stress or frustration.
- **Social Skills Development**: Group music therapy in schools fosters collaboration, communication, and social skills, particularly for students who may have difficulty engaging with peers. Activities like group singing, playing instruments, and songwriting encourage cooperation and self-expression.
- **Cognitive and Academic Support**: For students facing academic challenges, music therapy can help boost memory, attention, and organisational skills. Using music as a tool for learning, especially for those with dyslexia or other learning disabilities, can make academic content more accessible.
- **Inclusive Education**: Music therapy promotes inclusive education by allowing students of all abilities to participate in a shared, creative environment. Music-making activities provide a level playing field, enabling students with disabilities to engage in meaningful interactions with their peers.

Private Practice

In private practice, music therapists work with clients on a one-to-one basis or in small groups, offering highly individualised care. Common areas of focus in private practice include:

- **Mental Health**: Many music therapists in private practice specialise in mental health issues such as anxiety, depression, PTSD, and trauma. Therapeutic songwriting, improvisation, and guided imagery with music can help clients explore emotions, process traumatic experiences, and develop coping strategies.
- **Developmental and Neurological Disorders**: Clients with autism, cerebral palsy, or other developmental or neurological conditions benefit from tailored music therapy interventions that address communication, motor, and cognitive challenges.
- **Substance Abuse and Addiction Recovery**: In private practice, music therapy may be integrated into addiction recovery programmes to assist clients in understanding their emotions, improving self-awareness, and developing healthy coping mechanisms.
- **Elderly and Geriatric Care**: Music therapy is used with older adults, particularly those with Alzheimer's disease or other forms of dementia, to improve memory recall, reduce agitation, and promote socialisation. Familiar music from their past can evoke positive memories and emotions.
- **Stress Reduction and Personal Growth**: In some cases, clients seek out music therapy in private practice for general well-being, personal growth, or stress management. These

clients may not have a specific diagnosis but use music therapy as part of a holistic approach to self-care.

Each of these settings highlights the broad applicability of music therapy, demonstrating its potential to positively impact individuals across different stages of life and health conditions.

IX

Practical Application and Case Study of Music Therapy

Music therapy, the clinical use of music interventions to accomplish individualised goals, has found practical applications across diverse settings such as hospitals, rehabilitation centres, schools, and mental health facilities. This section will explore real-world case studies, treatment planning, and the importance of documentation in music therapy.

Case Study Examples

1. **Case Study 1: Music Therapy Intervention for Autism Spectrum Disorder (ASD)**
   - **Client**: A 7-year-old boy diagnosed with moderate ASD.
   - **Goal**: Improve social interaction and communication skills.
   - **Approach**: The music therapist utilised rhythmic activities such as drumming and call-and-response

singing to encourage turn-taking, joint attention, and verbal communication. These activities also reduced anxiety and helped the child express emotions.

- **Outcome**: After 12 weeks of sessions, the child demonstrated improved ability to initiate interactions, enhanced eye contact, and increased use of words to express needs.

2. **Case Study 2: Music Therapy for Stroke Rehabilitation**

- **Client**: A 62-year-old man recovering from a stroke with hemiplegia and aphasia.
- **Goal**: Regain motor coordination and improve speech abilities.
- **Approach**: Melodic intonation therapy (MIT) was employed to stimulate speech recovery, while rhythmic auditory stimulation (RAS) was used to help the client regain motor function. The therapist used music to facilitate hand movements and practice phrases rhythmically.
- **Outcome**: Over a 6-month period, the patient exhibited significant improvement in motor control, particularly in walking. His ability to form words increased, and his mood improved significantly.

3. **Case Study 3: Music Therapy in Palliative Care**

- **Client**: A 45-year-old woman with terminal cancer.
- **Goal**: Provide emotional support, reduce anxiety, and manage pain.
- **Approach**: Personalised music listening sessions based on the patient's musical preferences were integrated

into her care. Live music interventions, such as guitar playing and soft singing, were introduced to help with pain management and provide a comforting atmosphere.

- **Outcome**: The patient reported feeling more relaxed, with noticeable reductions in anxiety and perceived pain. Music therapy also supported the patient and her family in coping with end-of-life emotions.

Treatment Planning

In music therapy, treatment planning is highly individualised, involving assessment, goal-setting, and intervention design based on the client's needs.

1. **Assessment**: The therapist evaluates the client's physical, emotional, cognitive, and social needs through formal and informal assessments, interviews, and musical engagement. The client's background, preferences, and strengths are considered to create a holistic view.
   - ***Tools used***: Observations, standardised tests
   - ***Considerations***: Medical history, cognitive levels, emotional state, and responsiveness to music.
2. **Goal Setting**: Goals should be Specific, Measurable, Achievable, Relevant, and Time-bound. These goals might focus on improving communication skills, emotional expression, cognitive functioning, or physical rehabilitation.
   - ***For a child with ASD***: Increase non-verbal communication (e.g., gestures) by 50% in 3 months.

- ***For an elderly client with dementia***: Reduce agitation episodes during evening routines by 25% using music calming strategies over 6 weeks.

3. **Interventions**: These are selected based on the client's specific needs and are flexible. Interventions may include:
   - ***Receptive methods***: Guided music listening for relaxation, emotional exploration, or memory recall.
   - ***Active methods***: Singing, playing instruments, or improvisation to foster self-expression and coordination.
   - ***Movement to music***: To improve physical mobility or enhance body awareness.
4. **Evaluation and Adjustments**: Regular evaluations ensure progress is tracked, and the treatment plan is adjusted based on how the client is responding.

Documentation & Record Keeping

Proper documentation is essential in music therapy for tracking progress, maintaining accountability, and ensuring the continuity of care. It also serves as a communication tool among healthcare professionals and ensures adherence to professional and ethical standards.

Session Notes:

After each session, the therapist documents key observations, including:

Client's mood and engagement levels: Was the client calm, anxious or resistant?

Interventions used: Specific songs, instruments, or activities employed during the session.

Responses: How the client responded—both verbal and non-verbal reactions.

Progress towards goals: Document any milestones or improvements observed.

Progress Reports:

Periodic reports summarise the client's overall progress, challenges, and any necessary adjustments in the treatment plan. These reports often highlight:

- Goals met or exceeded.
- Recommendations for further therapy or alternative interventions.

1. **Client Logs & Assessment Records**:

   Comprehensive records, including initial assessments, regular session logs, and audio/video recordings (with consent), help create a full picture of the therapeutic process. These records may be used in research or to evaluate the effectiveness of the therapy.

2. **Collaboration Notes**:

   Documenting interactions with other healthcare professionals, such as doctors, physical therapists, or psychologists, is crucial for interdisciplinary care. These notes ensure that the music therapy interventions align with other treatments the client is receiving.

X

Music Therapy for Specific Populations

Children & Adolescence

Music therapy can significantly benefit children and adolescents in various contexts. Specific techniques are tailored to address emotional, behavioural, developmental, and trauma-related challenges.

Techniques for Emotional and Behavioural Issues

- **Improvisation**: Encourages self-expression by allowing children to play musical instruments freely, helping them process emotions and externalise inner conflicts.
- **Songwriting**: Facilitates the expression of feelings, enabling children to articulate emotions they may find difficult to express verbally.

- **Lyric Analysis**: Analysing the lyrics of songs can provide a way for children to reflect on their emotions, identify with certain themes, and gain insight into their emotional states.
- **Group Music-making**: Builds social skills and emotional regulation by promoting cooperation, turn-taking, and healthy interaction.
- **Rhythmic activities**: Drumming or rhythmic games help channel energy constructively, improving impulse control and reducing aggressive behaviours.

Techniques for Developmental Disorders

- **Structured Music Activities**: For children with autism or other developmental disorders, structured music-making can improve social skills, communication, and turn-taking.
- **Sensory Integration through Music**: Using instruments and movement to stimulate sensory processing can help children with sensory processing disorders or developmental delays.
- **Musical Play**: Engages children in a therapeutic setting through familiar songs and playful interactions, fostering language development, attention span, and motor skills.
- **Music and Movement**: Encourages sensory integration and motor development, often paired with structured activities that enhance communication and attention.
- **Interactive Music Play**: Creates a safe environment where children with developmental delays can practice social interactions and develop verbal and non-verbal communication skills.

- **Sensory Stimulation**: Engages children through varied musical textures, rhythms, and tones to address sensory sensitivities often present in developmental disorders.

Techniques for Trauma and Abuse

- **Musical Storytelling**: This technique helps children externalise their trauma by creating narratives through music. Allows children to explore their trauma in a safe, creative way, often by telling their story through song.
- **Safe Musical Space**: Creating a predictable and safe environment for music-making allows children to explore difficult emotions and reduce anxiety.
- **Music and Relaxation**: Using calming music for relaxation can help reduce hyperarousal symptoms often associated with trauma and PTSD in children.
- **Drumming Circles**: Helps children release pent-up energy and emotions, offering a non-verbal way to express feelings of anger, fear, or anxiety.
- **Music Listening and Relaxation**: Incorporates soothing music to help regulate emotions, manage stress, and create a sense of safety.
- **Guided Imagery with Music (GIM)**: Uses music to evoke images or memories that can help children process and verbalise their trauma.

Adults

Music therapy for adults is effective in addressing a variety of mental health issues, physical rehabilitation needs, and substance use disorders.

Techniques for Mental Health Disorders

- **Guided Imagery in Music (GIM)**: Adults listen to pre-recorded music while being guided through mental imagery, helping them access subconscious thoughts and emotions.
- **Drumming Circles**: Group drumming can enhance social connection, reduce anxiety, and improve mood in those with depression or anxiety disorders.
- **Songwriting and Lyric Writing**: Composing and performing songs can help individuals with mental health issues process their feelings, improve self-esteem, and foster emotional release. Supports self-reflection and emotional expression, offering a non-verbal outlet for feelings related to depression, anxiety, or other disorders.
- **Music-Mediated Mindfulness**: Combines mindfulness techniques with music to reduce anxiety, enhance emotional regulation, and foster relaxation.
- **Group Music Therapy**: Promotes social interaction and support among peers, building a sense of community, and reducing isolation.
- **Music-Assisted Relaxation**: Uses calming music to manage symptoms like anxiety, mood swings, and stress, particularly in patients with PTSD or generalised anxiety disorders.

Techniques for Physical Rehabilitation

- **Rhythmic Auditory Stimulation**: Enhances motor skills in stroke survivors, those with Parkinson's disease, or individuals recovering from traumatic brain injury, improving gait and movement.

- **Music-Assisted Movement**: Using music to prompt specific movements helps enhance physical rehabilitation for individuals with mobility issues.
- **Active Music Participation**: Playing instruments such as hand drums or keyboards engages motor skills, aiding in physical recovery and improving fine motor function.
- **Music-Supported Therapy (MST)**: Involves playing musical instruments to improve fine motor skills, hand-eye coordination, and overall motor function during physical rehabilitation.
- **Vocalisation and Singing**: Encourages breath control, speech production, and cognitive functioning in patients recovering from stroke or other physical impairments.
- **Therapeutic Drumming**: Engages the body in rhythm-based movement, enhancing motor coordination and physical endurance in rehabilitation settings.

Techniques for Substance Abuse

- **Group Music Therapy**: In a supportive group setting, music can facilitate communication and provide a non-verbal outlet for expressing struggles with addiction.
- **Music-Assisted Reflection**: Listening to and reflecting on songs can promote introspection and emotional healing for individuals dealing with substance abuse. Helps patients explore and identify feelings associated with addiction, often leading to greater self-awareness and emotional healing.

- **Motivational Music**: Using music to increase motivation for change, reinforcing, and enhancing coping skills.
- **Lyric Writing and Songwriting**: Allows patients to express their struggles with addiction, shame, or guilt through creative means.
- **Music-Mediated Relaxation and Mindfulness**: Aids in stress reduction, helping patients manage withdrawal symptoms and cravings.
- **Group Drumming Circles**: Promotes connection and builds a sense of community and support among patients in recovery, fostering social skills and emotional release.

Elderly

Music therapy for the elderly focuses on improving cognitive function, managing chronic illness, and providing comfort in palliative care.

Techniques for Cognitive Decline and Dementia

- **Familiar Music Listening**: Uses songs from the individual's past to stimulate memory recall, enhance communication, and improve mood in patients with dementia.
- **Music-Enhanced Reminiscence**: Music is used to evoke memories from the past, helping to maintain personal identity and emotional connection.
- **Movement to Music**: Dancing or gentle movement activities help improve physical health and cognitive function, even in individuals with cognitive decline. Incorporates rhythm-based movement to improve physical

coordination, flexibility, and balance, and boosts cognitive function through increased engagement.

- **Singing and Vocalisation**: Engages language centres in the brain, helping to improve speech, communication, and cognitive abilities in those with Alzheimer's or other forms of dementia.
- **Music-Evoked Autobiographical Memory**: Evokes personal memories through music to stimulate conversation, cognitive processing, and emotional connection.

Techniques for Chronic Illness

- **Live Music for Relaxation**: Providing live, calming music can reduce stress and anxiety in individuals dealing with chronic illness, improving overall quality of life. This live music session can be conducted at home or in a hospital setting. Live music played according to the individual's preferences helps to improve mood and create a positive atmosphere during long-term care.
- **Breath Control through Music**: Using music to guide breathing exercises can help manage symptoms in illnesses like COPD or heart disease.
- **Pain Management through Music**: Engaging patients in active music-making or listening can reduce the perception of pain and discomfort. Rhythmic patterns and calming melodies help to modulate the perception of pain and promote relaxation.
- **Music-Assisted Relaxation**: Reduces pain, anxiety, and depression associated with chronic illness, often using calming or meditative music.

Techniques for Palliative Care

- **Music for Emotional Support**: In end-of-life care, music can provide emotional comfort, helping patients and their families process grief and transition.
- **Live Therapeutic Music**: Offers comfort and emotional support, creating a peaceful environment for patients in the final stages of life.
- **Music for Emotional Expression**: Provides an outlet for patients to process feelings of fear, grief, or loss, especially those nearing the end of life.
- **Music-Assisted Life Review**: Helps patients reflect on their life experiences through familiar songs, promoting a sense of closure and emotional peace.
- **Music-Assisted Relaxation and Imagery**: Encourages relaxation and alleviates anxiety, pain, and discomfort, using soft, calming music tailored to the individual's preferences.

Each of these techniques is applied by certified music therapists based on the specific needs of the population they are working with, fostering healing and improving quality of life across various age groups and challenges.

Music Therapy in ADHD

Case Study Overview:

Patient: A 10-year-old male diagnosed with ADHD (Attention-Deficit/Hyperactivity Disorder) with severe hyperactivity, impulsivity, and concentration issues.

Treatment Plan:

- **Goal**: Improve focus, enhance self-control, and reduce hyperactivity through music-based interventions.
- **Methods Used**:

  Rhythmic Entrainment: The therapist used rhythmic drumming activities, which required the child to maintain a consistent beat. This helped in enhancing attention span and impulse control.

  Structured Musical Activities: Activities involved listening to calm music (such as classical or slow tempo) to soothe the child's hyperactive tendencies.

  Interactive Music-Making: Engaged the patient in playing musical instruments like maracas and tambourines, which helped redirect his impulsive energy in a controlled manner.

Outcomes:

- Over the course of three months, the child's ability to focus on tasks improved notably.
- Hyperactivity and impulsive outbursts decreased by 40%, according to parent reports.

- The child learned to use music independently as a calming tool when he felt overwhelmed or overly energetic.

Conclusion: Music therapy provided a non-pharmacological tool to support ADHD treatment by offering a way to channel energy productively and improving self-regulation.

Music Therapy in Depression

Case Study Overview:

Patient: A 32-year-old female diagnosed with major depressive disorder, presenting with low energy, lack of motivation, and feelings of hopelessness.

Treatment Plan:

- **Goal**: To improve mood, increase motivation, and provide emotional expression through music.
- **Methods Used**:

  Lyric Analysis: Sessions involved analysing the lyrics of emotionally relevant songs. The patient identified with the struggles and emotions in the songs, which helped her process her own feelings.

  Songwriting: She began composing her own songs as a way to externalise her thoughts, giving her an outlet for emotional expression and catharsis.

  Active Listening and Music Selection: Therapists encouraged her to listen to uplifting music and created a personalised playlist that matched her emotional states.

Outcomes:

- After six months of therapy, the patient reported a noticeable improvement in mood and energy levels. Her Beck Depression Inventory (BDI) score reduced by 30%.

- She also began to use songwriting as a regular form of emotional release, resulting in a reduction in her negative thought patterns.

Conclusion: Music therapy served as an effective adjunct to traditional psychotherapy by providing a safe and creative avenue for emotional expression, leading to improved mood and coping mechanisms.

Music Therapy in PTSD (Post-Traumatic Stress Disorder)

Case Study Overview:

Patient: A 45-year-old combat veteran diagnosed with PTSD, experiencing flashbacks, hypervigilance, and anxiety related to traumatic events.

Treatment Plan:

- **Goal**: To reduce anxiety and flashbacks, enhance emotional regulation, and foster relaxation.
- **Methods Used**:

  Improvisational Music: The therapist provided a range of instruments and encouraged the patient to improvise music that represented their inner emotional turmoil. This allowed for a non-verbal exploration of traumatic memories.

  Guided Imagery with Music (GIM): During the sessions, the therapist guided the patient to imagine peaceful scenarios while listening to specially woven calming music. This technique helped the patient dissociate from traumatic memories and focus on positive mental imagery.

  Drumming Circles: Drumming circles were employed to encourage emotional expression, grounding and social connection.

Outcomes:

- Over the course of five months, the patient reported a reduction in the frequency of flashbacks and intrusive memories.
- His anxiety levels decreased significantly, and he was better able to sleep at night.
- Participating in drumming circles also fostered a sense of community and reduced his feelings of isolation.

Conclusion: Music therapy proved effective in reducing PTSD symptoms by providing a way for the patient to process trauma in a safe, non-verbal environment. The guided imagery helped with emotional regulation, and the community aspect of drumming circles reduced isolation.

Music Therapy in Cancer Palliative Care

Case Study Overview:

Patient: A 65-year-old female with stage IV breast cancer, receiving palliative care. She experienced chronic pain, anxiety and existential distress.

Treatment Plan:

- **Goal**: To alleviate pain, reduce anxiety, and enhance quality of life during palliative care.
- **Methods Used**:

  Receptive Music Therapy: The patient engaged in passive listening to her favourite music (soft classical music), which helped in lowering anxiety levels during chemotherapy and other treatments.

  Music-Assisted Relaxation: Music was paired with guided deep breathing and relaxation techniques to help manage her chronic pain and provide a sense of comfort and calm.

  Life Review and Legacy Songwriting: The patient collaborated with the music therapist to create a "legacy" song that reflected her life's journey and values. This was recorded and given to her family.

Outcomes:

- The patient reported a significant decrease in perceived pain levels during therapy sessions, measured through a visual analog scale.

- Her overall anxiety and distress were reduced, leading to better sleep and improved mood.
- The creation of the legacy song gave her a sense of closure and meaning, improving her emotional well-being in her final months.

Conclusion: In cancer palliative care, music therapy offered both psychological and physical benefits. It helped reduce pain and anxiety while enhancing emotional well-being, providing the patient with an opportunity to leave a meaningful legacy.

XI

Introduction to Participatory Music

Participatory music activities and games are a cornerstone of music therapy, offering a unique and engaging approach to treatment. Unlike passive listening, these activities involve clients directly in the music-making process, fostering self-expression, social connection, and skill development.

Participatory music activities are built on the principle of active engagement, where the client is a co-creator rather than a recipient of the therapy. The primary therapeutic goals include:

Improving Social Skills: Group activities like drumming circles or musical improvisation can enhance communication, cooperation, and empathy. Clients learn to listen to others, take turns, and contribute to a shared experience.

Enhancing Emotional Expression: Through instruments, voice, or movement, clients can explore and express emotions in a safe, non-verbal way. For example, a client may use the intensity of a drum beat to express anger or a soft melody to convey sadness.

Developing Cognitive and Motor Skills: Activities like rhythm games or learning a simple song can improve memory, attention, and fine and gross motor coordination. This is particularly beneficial for individuals with developmental or neurological conditions.

Building Self-Esteem and Confidence: Successfully participating in a musical activity, whether it's playing a simple chord or singing a phrase, can provide a significant boost to a client's sense of accomplishment and self-worth.

Here are some elaborate ways to use music in therapy sessions, structured by specific therapeutic goals.

Introductory Session

The introductory session sets the tone for the therapeutic relationship. Music can be used to build rapport and create a safe space.

Musical Greeting: The therapist can play a simple, gentle melody on an instrument like a guitar or ukulele as the client enters. This non-verbal greeting can be more comforting than a spoken one, especially for clients who are anxious or have difficulty with verbal communication. The greeting can be personalised over time, becoming a special ritual.

Musical Icebreaker: Use a "pass the pulse" activity. A small percussion instrument (like an egg shaker or rhythm stick) is passed around the circle. Each person adds a sound or short rhythmic pattern, and the group responds. This activity is non-threatening and gets everyone engaged without the pressure of speaking. It helps to establish a sense of group cohesion and shared rhythm.

Creating a "Musical Name": Ask each person to choose an instrument that represents their mood or personality and play a short sound. This is a creative and non-confrontational way for people to introduce themselves. The therapist can then "respond" musically to each person's sound, showing that they are listening and validating their expression.

Awareness of Surroundings & Focus

Music can be used to help clients ground themselves in the present moment and become more aware of their environment.

Auditory Scavenger Hunt: The therapist plays a variety of sounds (e.g., a bell, a wooden block, a shaker) and asks the client to identify the source of each sound. This sharpens auditory attention and encourages the client to focus on their immediate surroundings.

"Sound-Walk": In a group setting, everyone walks around the room, paying close attention to the sounds they hear (e.g., footsteps, breathing, the hum of an air conditioner). The group then comes back together and recreates these sounds using instruments, creating a shared "soundscape" of the environment.

Guided Listening: Play a piece of music with distinct layers of instruments (e.g., a classical piece with strings, woodwinds, and percussion). Ask the client to close their eyes and focus on listening for one specific instrument at a time. This activity improves sustained attention and helps clients to filter out extraneous auditory information.

Scanning Your Mind & Memory

Music has a powerful link to memory and can be used to help clients explore their inner world.

"Sound Portrait": Ask the client to think of a specific feeling, memory, or person and then select instruments to create a "sound portrait" of it. This process helps them to externalise their inner thoughts and emotions in a non-verbal way. The therapist can then ask guiding questions about the choices, such as "What does the loud drum in your sound portrait represent?"

Musical Mind Map: The therapist plays different types of music (e.g., a calm piece, an energetic piece, a nostalgic piece). After each one, the client writes down the first thoughts, memories, or feelings that come to mind. This is a form of free association that uses music as a prompt.

Life Soundtrack: Clients create a playlist of songs that represent different periods or significant events in their lives. The therapist can then use this "life soundtrack" as a framework for exploring their personal narrative, discussing pivotal moments, and identifying recurring themes.

Imagery and Music

Music can be a powerful catalyst for a client's imagination and visualisation.

Guided Imagery: The therapist plays a piece of instrumental music while guiding the client through a vivid, story-like visualisation. For example, a calm piece might accompany a scene of walking through a peaceful forest, while an upbeat, adventurous piece might be used for a journey over mountains. This can be used for relaxation, stress reduction, and to help clients practice coping skills in an imagined scenario.

Musical Drawing: The client listens to a piece of music and is asked to draw or paint whatever comes to mind without consciously trying to make sense of it. The focus is on translating the sounds, rhythms, and emotions of the music directly onto the paper. This activity is excellent for clients who find it difficult to articulate their feelings verbally.

Music for Movement

Movement and music are intrinsically linked and can be used to improve physical and emotional well-being.

Rhythmic Entrainment: The therapist plays a steady beat and encourages the client to move in time with the music (e.g., tapping their foot, nodding their head, or walking). This simple act can improve motor coordination and a sense of internal rhythm.

Musical Freeze Dance: A fun and effective activity, the therapist plays music for a short time and then stops. Everyone must freeze in place. This helps with impulse control and the ability to start and stop an action on command, which can be useful for individuals with ADHD or other attention issues.

Emotional Motion: The therapist plays music that evokes different emotions (e.g., a fast, dissonant piece for anger; a slow, flowing piece for sadness) and asks the client to move their body in a way that reflects the emotion they feel from the music. This helps clients connect their physical self with their emotional state.

Music Therapy in Puzzles

Puzzles and games can be made more engaging and therapeutic with the addition of music.

Musical Puzzle: Create a puzzle where each piece is a picture of an instrument or a musical note. When the client places a piece correctly, a corresponding sound can be played. This reinforces a sense of accomplishment and makes the activity more interactive.

Collaborative Rhythm Puzzle: Each group member is given a simple rhythmic pattern on a card. The goal is to piece together their individual patterns to create a larger, cohesive rhythm. This activity improves teamwork, communication, and the ability to work towards a shared goal.

Emotion and Motion with Music

This is a core component of music therapy, linking internal feelings to external expression.

Emotional Playlist: The therapist and client create a playlist of songs that represent different emotions they want to work on (e.g., a song for feeling anxious, a song for feeling happy, a song for feeling calm). The client can use this playlist as a tool to help them identify and validate their feelings as they arise.

"Sounding" an Emotion: The therapist asks the client to use a drum or another instrument to play what "anger" sounds like, what "joy" sounds like, or what "sadness" sounds like. This allows the client to externalise their feelings in a safe and contained way. The therapist can then engage with the client about their musical choices, asking questions like, "What made the sound for anger so loud?" This facilitates a deeper conversation about the client's emotions.

XII

References

General Texts on Music Therapy

1. Bunt, L., & Stige, B. (2014). **Music Therapy: An Art Beyond Words**. Routledge.
2. Bruscia, K. E. (2014). **Defining Music Therapy** (3rd ed.). Barcelona Publishers.
3. Aigen, K. (2013). **The Study of Music Therapy: Current Issues and Concepts**. Routledge.
4. Wheeler, B. L. (2015). **Music Therapy Handbook**. The Guilford Press.
5. Bruscia, K. E. (1998). **The Dynamics of Music Psychotherapy**. Barcelona Publishers.

Research Papers on Music Therapy

6. Amir, D. (1993). **Moments of Insight in the Process of Music Therapy**. Music Therapy, 12(1), 85-100.

7. Loewy, J. (2000). **Music Therapy in the NICU**. Neonatal Network, 19(3), 41-46.
8. Edwards, J. (2016). **Music Therapy and Parent–Infant Bonding**. Oxford University Press.
9. Dileo, C. (1999). **Music Therapy and Medicine: Theoretical and Clinical Applications**. American Music Therapy Association.
10. Wigram, T., & Elefant, C. (2009). **Music Therapy for Children and Adults with Severe Disabilities**. Oxford University Press.
11. Thaut, M. H. (2005). **Rhythm, Music, and the Brain: Scientific Foundations and Clinical Applications**. Routledge.
12. Sacks, O. (2007). **Musicophilia: Tales of Music and the Brain**. Knopf.
13. Magee, W. L. (2019). **Music Technology in Therapeutic and Health Settings**. Jessica Kingsley Publishers.
14. Sarkamo, T., Tervaniemi, M., & Huotilainen, M. (2013). **Music and Rehabilitation: Neurological Approaches**. Annals of the New York Academy of Sciences, 1303, 1-15.
15. Boso, M., Politi, P., & Barale, F. (2006). **Neurophysiology and Neurobiology of the Musical Experience**. Annals of the New York Academy of Sciences, 1060, 1-30.
16. Gold, C., Wigram, T., & Elefant, C. (2006). **Music Therapy for Autistic Spectrum Disorder**. Cochrane Database of Systematic Reviews, CD004381.

17. Katagiri, J. (2009). **The Effect of Background Music and Song Texts on the Emotional Understanding of Children with Autism**. Journal of Music Therapy, 46(1), 15-31.
18. Wigram, T. (2002). **Indications in Music Therapy: Evidence from Assessment that Can Identify the Expectations of Music Therapy as a Treatment for Autistic Spectrum Disorder (ASD)**. British Journal of Music Therapy, 16(1), 11-28.
19. Whipple, J. (2004). **Music in Intervention for Children and Adolescents with Autism: A Meta-Analysis**. Journal of Music Therapy, 41(2), 90-106.
20. Geretsegger, M., Elefant, C., Mossler, K., & Gold, C. (2014). **Music Therapy for People with Autism Spectrum Disorder**. Cochrane Database of Systematic Reviews, CD004381.
21. Callaghan, C. C. (2013). **Music Therapy in Palliative Care: New Voices**. Oxford University Press.
22. Dileo, C., & Loewy, J. V. (2005). **Music Therapy at the End of Life**. Jeffrey Books.
23. Magill, L. (2009). **The Meaning of the Music: The Role of Music in Palliative Care Music Therapy as Perceived by Bereaved Caregivers of Advanced Cancer Patients**. American Journal of Hospice and Palliative Medicine, 26(1), 33-39.
24. Hilliard, R. E. (2005). **Music Therapy in Hospice and Palliative Care: A Review of the Empirical Data**. Evidence-Based Complementary and Alternative Medicine, 2(2), 173-178.

25. Krout, R. E. (2003). **The Effects of Single-Session Music Therapy Interventions on the Observed and Self-Reported Levels of Pain Control, Physical Comfort, and Relaxation of Hospice Patients.** American Journal of Hospice and Palliative Medicine, 20(2), 129-136.

26. Bonde, L. O. (2007). **Music Therapy and Anxiety**. In P. Aldridge (Ed.), *Music Therapy in Mental Health*. Jessica Kingsley Publishers.

27. Silverman, M. J. (2011). **The Effect of Music Therapy on Anxiety in Patients with Schizophrenia**. Journal of Music Therapy, 48(3), 285-306.

28. Hadley, S., & Yancy, G. (2011). **Therapeutic Uses of Rap and Hip-Hop**. Routledge.

29. Erkkilä, J., Punkanen, M., & Ala-Ruona, E. (2011). **Individual Music Therapy for Depression: Randomised Controlled Trial**. British Journal of Psychiatry, 199(2), 132-139.

30. Moore, K. S. (2013). **A Systematic Review on the Neural Effects of Music on Emotion Regulation: Implications for Music Therapy Practice**. Journal of Music Therapy, 50(3), 198-242.

31. Raglio, A., Gianelli, M. V., & Fonte, C. (2015). **Music Therapy for Individuals with Dementia: Areas of Interventions and Research Perspectives.** Complementary Therapies in Clinical Practice, 21(2), 75-80.

32. Clare, L., & Woods, R. T. (2004). **Cognitive Rehabilitation and Cognitive Training for Early-Stage**

Alzheimer's Disease and Vascular Dementia. Cochrane Database of Systematic Reviews, CD003260.

33. Davidson, J. W., McNamara, B., & Rosenwax, L. K. (2014). **Use of Music or Music Therapy in the Dying Phase.** Journal of Palliative Care, 30(2), 100-105.
34. Ledger, A., & Baker, F. (2007). **An Investigation of Long-Term Effects of Group Music Therapy on Agitation Levels of People with Alzheimer's Disease.** Aging & Mental Health, 11(3), 330-338.
35. Ridder, H. M., Stige, B., Qvale, L. G., & Gold, C. (2013). **Individual Music Therapy for Agitation in Dementia.** Dementia, 12(4), 1-14.
36. Stige, B. (2002). **Culture-Centered Music Therapy.** Barcelona Publishers.
37. Ruud, E. (1998). **Music Therapy: Improvisation, Communication, and Culture.** Barcelona Publishers.
38. Ansdell, G. (1995). **Music for Life: Aspects of Creative Music Therapy with Adult Clients.** Jessica Kingsley Publishers.
39. Pavlicevic, M. (1997). **Music Therapy in Context: Music, Meaning, and Relationship.** Jessica Kingsley Publishers.
40. DeNora, T. (2000). **Music in Everyday Life.** Cambridge University Press.
41. Bensimon, M., Amir, D., & Wolf, Y. (2008). **Drumming Through Trauma: Music Therapy with Post-Traumatic Soldiers.** The Arts in Psychotherapy, 35(1), 34-48.

42. Orth, J., & Verbovsek, T. (2014). **Music Therapy in Trauma Treatment and Disaster Relief**. Voices: A World Forum for Music Therapy, 14(1).
43. Gooding, L. F. (2017). **Music Therapy Interventions for Traumatic Brain Injury**. Music Therapy Perspectives, 35(2), 125-136.
44. Carr, C., d'Ardenne, P., & Sloboda, A. (2012). **Group Music Therapy for Patients with Post-Traumatic Stress Disorder**. The Arts in Psychotherapy, 39(2), 190-196.
45. Beck, B. D., Messel, C., & Meyer, S. L. (2018). **Music Therapy for Stress and Anxiety in Traumatized Refugees**. European Journal of Trauma & Dissociation, 2(1), 45-52.
46. Magee, W. L., & O'Kelly, J. (2015). **Music Therapy and Electronic Technology**. In B. Wheeler (Ed.), *Music Therapy Handbook*. The Guilford Press.
47. Knight, A., & Krout, R. (2016). **Music Technology Use in Therapeutic Settings**. Music Therapy Perspectives, 34(1), 1-8.
48. Turry, A. (2016). **Music Technology and Clinical Improvisation in Music Therapy**. International Journal of Music Therapy, 23(4), 328-337.
49. Magee, W. L. (2013). **Music Therapy and Neurological Rehabilitation**. Routledge.
50. Crowe, B. J., & Rio, R. (2004). **Implications of Technology in Music Therapy Practice and Research for the Next Decade**. Music Therapy Perspectives, 22(1), 39-44.

51. Bonny, H. L. (2002). *Music and consciousness: The evolution of guided imagery and music (GIM)*. Barcelona Publishers.
52. Chanda, M. L., & Levitin, D. J. (2013). The neurochemistry of music. *Trends in Cognitive Sciences, 17*(4), 179–193. https://doi.org/10.1016/j.tics.2013.02.007
53. Geretsegger, M., Elefant, C., Mössler, K. A., & Gold, C. (2014). Music therapy for people with autism spectrum disorder. *Cochrane Database of Systematic Reviews*, (6). https://doi.org/10.1002/14651858.CD004381.pub3
54. Gupta, U., & Gupta, M. (2005). Psychophysiological effects of music in stress management. *Indian Journal of Physiology and Pharmacology, 49*(2), 163–169.
55. Harvard Health Publishing. (2020). *Music and health: What the science says*. Harvard Medical School.
56. Kakar, S. (1991). *Shamans, mystics, and doctors: A psychological inquiry into India and its healing traditions*. University of Chicago Press.
57. Koelsch, S. (2010). Towards a neural basis of music-evoked emotions. *Trends in Cognitive Sciences, 14*(3), 131–137. https://doi.org/10.1016/j.tics.2010.01.002
58. Kumar, A. M., Telles, S., & Nagendra, H. R. (1999). Meditation on the OM sound: EEG and respiratory changes. *International Journal of Neuroscience, 100*(1–4), 77–86. https://doi.org/10.3109/00207459908994796
59. Nagendra, H. R., & Telles, S. (1997). Music therapy for stress management. *Journal of Indian Psychology, 15*(1), 15–21.

60. Särkämö, T., Tervaniemi, M., Laitinen, S., Forsblom, A., Soinila, S., Mikkonen, M.,... & Hietanen, M. (2014). Cognitive, emotional, and social benefits of regular musical activities in early dementia: Randomized controlled study. *The Gerontologist, 54*(4), 634–650. https://doi.org/10.1093/geront/gnt100

61. Thakur, M. K., & Joshi, A. (2012). Effect of Indian classical music (Raga Desi and Raga Bhairavi) on blood pressure and heart rate in healthy young individuals. *Indian Journal of Physiology and Pharmacology, 56*(2), 174–178.

62. Trappe, H. J. (2012). Role of music in intensive care medicine. *Intensive Care Medicine, 38*(4), 608–610. https://doi.org/10.1007/s00134-011-2445-3

www.ingramcontent.com/pod-product-compliance
Lightning Source LLC
LaVergne TN
LVHW090329210926
848480LV00004B/1355
* 9 7 9 8 9 0 0 0 7 8 3 5 9 *